Contents

The sea

Large parts of the Earth are covered by sea. The sea is home to many different animals.

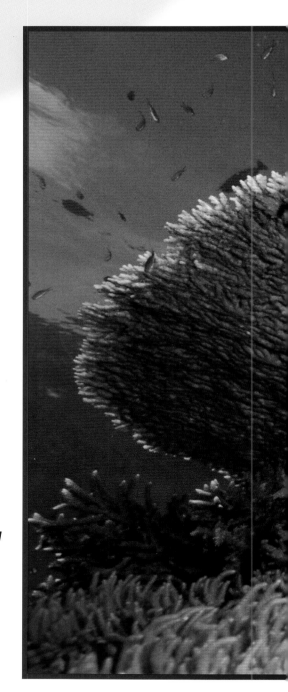

▶ *Coral reefs are made in warm sea water. Fish feed on plants and animals that live on the reef.*

Sea Animals

Claire Llewellyn

FRANKLIN WATTS
LONDON·SYDNEY

First published in 2004
by Franklin Watts
338 Euston Road
London NW1 3BH

Franklin Watts Australia
Level 17/207 Kent Street
Sydney NSW 2000

Series advisor: Gill Matthews, non-fiction literacy consultant and Inset trainer
Editor: Rachel Cooke
Designer: James Marks
Acknowledgements: Fred Bavendam/Still Pictures: 13b. Edward Bent/Ecoscene: 15b.Phillip Colla/Ecoscene: 2, 10, 12, 14, 22br, 23tl. Jeff Collett/Ecoscene: 1, 9. S. Davis/Still Pictures: 16. Digital Vision: front cover, 19, 21, 23tr. Reinhard Dirsherl/Ecoscene: 8, 11tl, 11r. Claude Guihard/Still Pictures: 17. Bruno Pambour/Still Pictures: 6. Edward Parker/Still Pictures: 20. Robert Pickett/Ecoscene: 15t. Jeffrey Rotman/Still Pictures: 13t. Peter Tatton/Ecoscene: 4-5, 22cl. Roger Tidman/FLPA: 7. Visual & Written/Ecoscene: 18.

A CIP catalogue record for this book is available from the British Library.

ISBN: 978 0 7496 8122 7

Printed in Malaysia

Franklin Watts is a division of Hachette Children's Books, an Hachette Livre UK company.

As well as fish, what other animals live in the sea?

By the shore

Some sea animals live by the shore. Many of them live inside shells.

▶ *A crab's shell protects its soft body.*

This bird uses its long beak to open shells and eat the animals inside.

Sea animals with shells are called shellfish. After shellfish die, we often find their empty shells on the beach.

In the water

All sorts of fish live in the water. They come in many shapes and sizes.

◀ *A huge manta ray is up to 6 metres wide – over twice as wide as a bus.*

▲ These two fish have very different shapes.

Fish live in different parts of the sea. Some live in deep water. Others stay near the shore.

▶ A seahorse is a fish that swims upright.

On the seabed

Many animals live on the seabed. They move around looking for food.

An octopus moves on its suckers.

There is food at the bottom of the sea. Dead plants and animals sink down to the seabed – so do the leftovers of other animals' meals.

▲ *A sea slug slides along the seabed.*

Moving in water

Many sea animals swim with flippers and fins. Others just float in the water.

Sea lions have flippers to push them through the water.

▲ Barracuda fish have fins. Their long, thin bodies cut quickly through the water.

Next time you have a bath, push your hand through the water – first with your fingers open, then closed. Which gives a better push against the water? Which is more like a flipper?

▶ A jellyfish floats wherever the sea takes it.

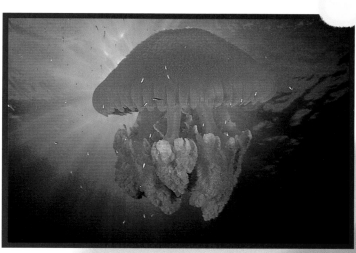

Finding food

There is plenty of food to eat in the sea. A lot of it is very, very tiny.

Whale sharks gulp down tiny animals.

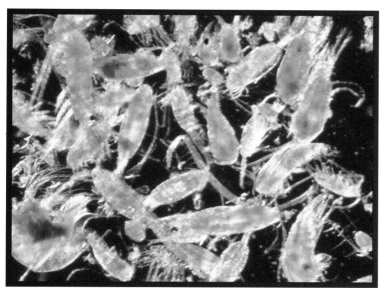

◀ These tiny sea animals can only be seen through a magnifying glass.

A whale shark does not have teeth. It has filters that strain food out of the water.

▶ Puffins dive for fish.

Staying alive

Sea animals do not want to be eaten. They have different ways of staying alive.

▶ *Fish are harder to catch if they swim together in a shoal.*

A flounder is a flat fish. It is hard to see.

Imagine that you were hiding in the sea. What sort of hiding places would you look for? How could you make yourself hard to see?

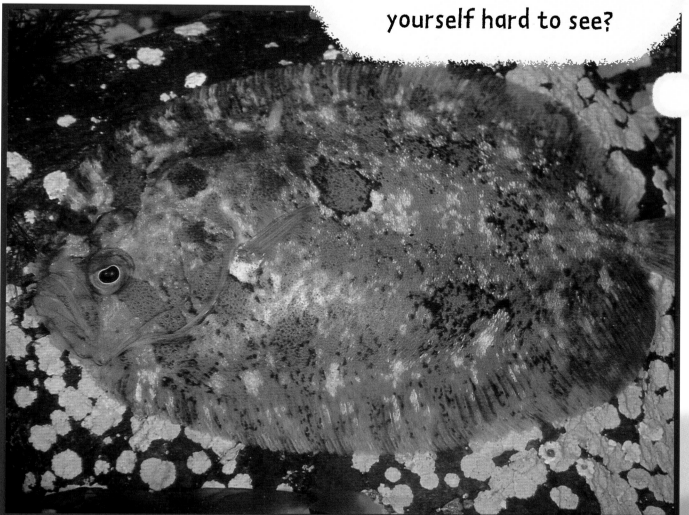

Breathing in water

All animals need to breathe to stay alive. They do this in different ways.

▶ *A fish uses its gills to breathe under water.*

gills

Most people can hold their breath for about 1 minute. A dolphin can hold its breath under water for about 10 minutes.

A dolphin has no gills. It must come up to the surface to breathe.

Sea animals in danger

Many sea animals are in danger. We need to protect them.

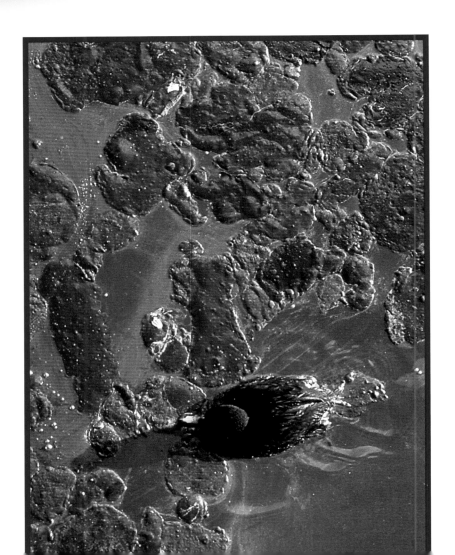

▶ *Dirty water harms sea animals.*

Fishermen are banned from catching sea animals that are in danger.

▲ *We like to eat fish, but we must not catch too many.*

I know that...

1 Many animals live in the sea.

2 Some sea animals live by the seashore.

3 Some sea animals live in the water or on the seabed.

4 Many sea animals have fins and flippers to help them swim.

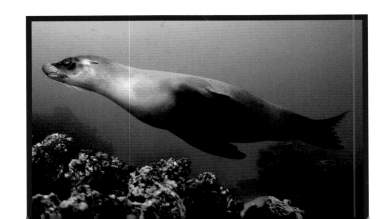

5 Sea animals feed on plants or on other animals.

6 Sea animals have different ways of staying alive.

7 Most sea animals can breathe under water.

8 Some sea animals breathe air at the surface.

9 Sea animals are in danger from dirty water and fishing.

Index

About this book

I Know That! is designed to introduce children to the process of gathering information and using reference books, one of the key skills needed to begin more formal learning at school. For this reason, each book's structure reflects the information books children will use later in their learning career – with key information in the main text and additional facts and ideas in the captions. The panels give an opportunity for further activities, ideas or discussions. The contents page and index are helpful reference guides.

The language is carefully chosen to be accessible to children just beginning to read. Illustrations support the text but also give information in their own right; active consideration and discussion of images is another key referencing skill. The main aim of the series is to build confidence - showing children how much they already know and giving them the ability to gather new information for themselves. With this in mind, the *I know that...* section at the end of the book is a simple way for children to revisit what they already know as well as what they have learnt from reading the book.